from the
HEART
25

Great Country Love Songs

Edited by Milton Okun

Contents

4...I Swear

8...Where've You Been

12...Love Can Build A Bridge

17...A Few Good Things Remain

21...Deeper Than The Holler

24...Longer

29...Part Of Me

32...Annie's Song

36...Love Is Strong

40...Love Chooses You

45...She Is His Only Need

Compiled by Len Handler
Production: Daniel Rosenbaum/Rana Bernhardt
Art Direction: Rosemary Cappa-Jenkins
Director of Music: Mark Phillips

52...The Battle Hymn Of Love

56...The Calm At The Center Of My Storm

60...'Til The Mountains Disappear

64...Unanswered Prayers

69...Lines Around Your Eyes

72...Like I Used To Do

78...Lady

82...I'll Leave This World Loving You

88...I Won't Take Less Than Your Love

94...Forever And Ever, Amen

98...Goin' Gone

102...I Know Where Love Lives

107...This Shirt

114...I Should Be With You

I Swear

Words and Music by
Frank J. Myers and Gary Baker

F   G   Am   F
ing on___ your mind.___ But you can be sure___ I know___ my part.___
___ with these___ two hands.___ And we'll hang some mem - 'ries on___ the wall.

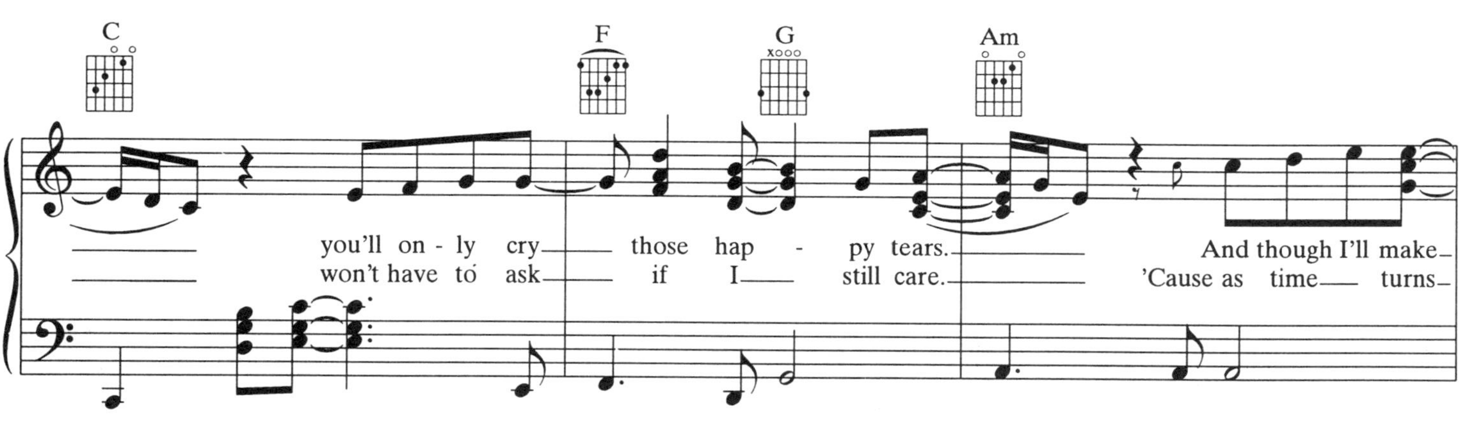

Gsus4   G   C   F/A   G/B
'Cause I'll___ stand be - side___ you through___ the years;
And when___ there's sil - ver in___ your hair,

C   F   G   Am
you'll on - ly cry___ those hap - py tears.___ And though I'll make___
won't have to ask___ if I still care.___ 'Cause as time___ turns___

C/G   D/F#   Gsus4   G
mis - takes,___ I'll nev - er break___ your heart.___
the page,___ my love won't___ age___ at all.___
I swear,-

C   Am7   Em7
by the moon   and the stars   in the sky,   I'll be there.
F   G   C   Am7
I swear,   like a shad - ow that's by   your side,
Em7   F   G   Dm7
I'll be there.   For bet - ter or worse,   till
Gsus4   G   Dm7   To Coda   1. Gsus4   G
death do us part,   I'll love you with ev - e - ry beat   of my heart,   I swear.
C   Am   Em7   F/G   G

2.
Gsus4   G   C   Am7
of my heart, I swear.
Em7   Gsus4   G   C
Am   Em7   F/G   G
D.S. al Coda
I swear
Gsus4   G   C
Coda
of my heart, I swear.
Am   F   G   C
I swear.
rit.

Where've You Been

Words and Music by
Don Henry and Jon Vezner

C/G   G   F#m7(b5)   B7
dis - be - lief   she   sighed   and __ said,
storm - y   eve - ning   he   wheeled   was __ late.
Then   one   day   they   wheeled   him __ in.

Am   G/B
"In   man - y   dreams   I've   held ______   you   near ______
Her   fright - ened   tears   fell   to ______   the   floor ______
He   held   her   hand   and   stroked __   her   head. ______

C   G/B   Am   D7sus   D7
but   now   at   last   you're   real - ly   here." __
un - til   his   key   turned   in ___   the   door. __
In   a   frag - ile   voice ___   she   said, __

G   Em7   C   Cmaj7
Where have you been? ___ I've looked for you for - ev - er and a ___
G   Em   C
To Coda
___ day. ___ Where have you been? ___
Em   D7/F#   1. G   2. G
I'm just not my - self when you're a - way. ___ way. ___
C   D/F#   G   Cmaj7
They'd nev - er spent a night ___ a - part. ___ For

Em7
C
six - ty years she heard him snore.___ Now they're in hos -
G/B Am D7 G/D D7
D.S. al Coda
- pi - tal ___ in sep-'rate beds on dif-f'rent floors. _
G Em C
CODA
Where have you been? _______ I'm just not my- self when you're a -
Em7 G/D D7 C(add9)
way. ______ No, I'm just not my-self when you're a - way.
rit.
rit.

Love Can Build A Bridge

Words and Music by
Paul Overstreet, Naomi Judd
and John Jarvis

* Recorded a half step lower.

Fsus2   C/G   G7sus4   G7   Chorus C   F
all your hopes— are sink-ing,   let me show you what love—means.   Love   can   build   a
er.
G7   Dm   G7/B   C   F   G
bridge   be-tween   your   heart   and   mine.
C   C/E   F   1. C/G   G7
To Coda
Love   can   build   a   bridge,   don't you think— it's time?—   Don't   you   think— it's time?—
C add 2   Dm7sus4/C   C add 2

Dm7sus4/C
2. C/G   G7   C   F
I would __ Don't you think__ it's time?__
G7   Dm   G7/B   C   F   G
C   C/E   F   C/G   G7
C   Am   G7/B   C
When we stand to-geth - er,___ it's our fin - est hour.___ We can do__

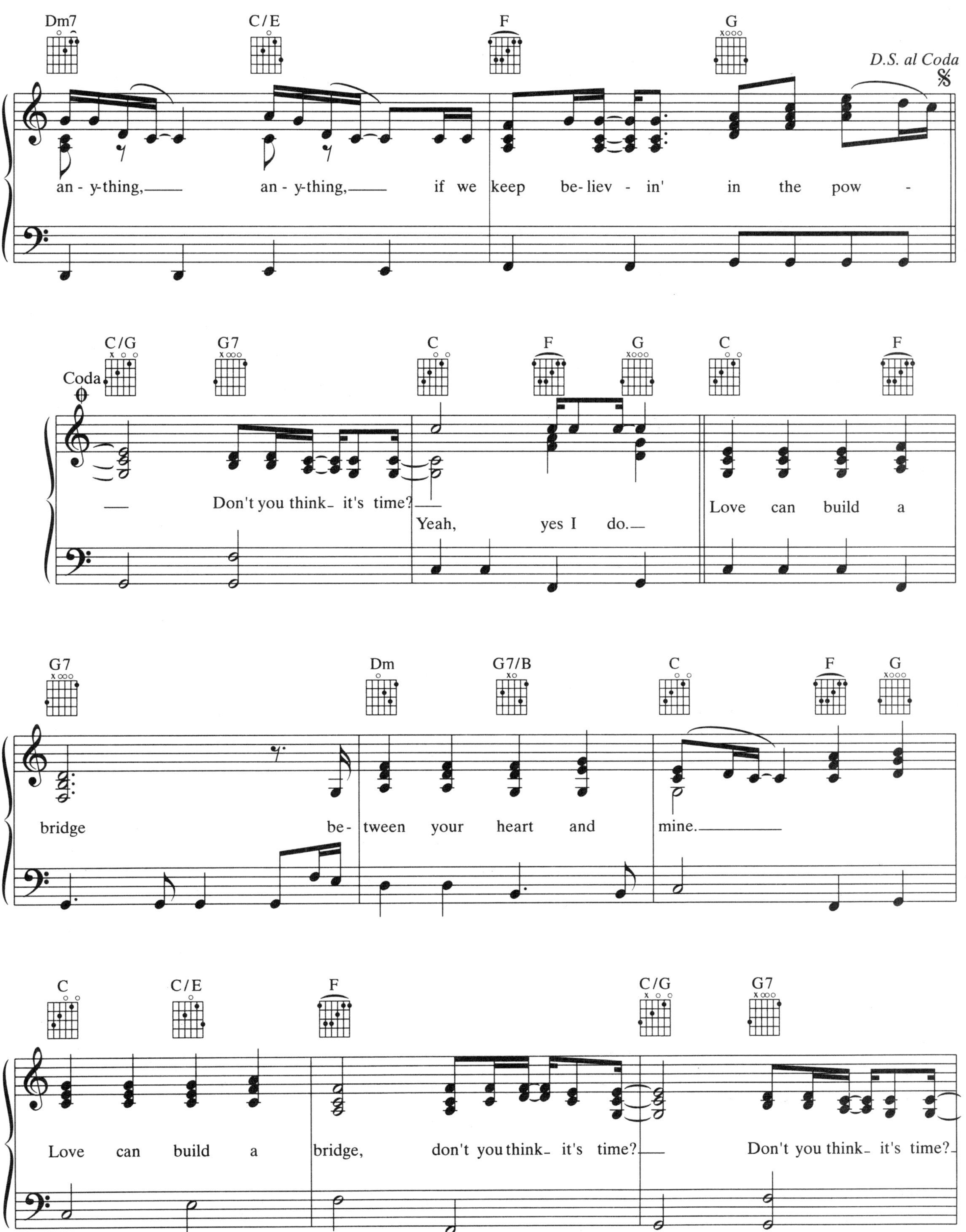

Dm7
C/E
F
G
D.S. al Coda
an - y-thing, ____ an - y-thing, ____ if we keep be- liev - in' in the pow -
C/G
G7
C
F
G
C
F
Coda
____ Don't you think_ it's time? ____
Yeah, yes I do. ____
Love can build a
G7
Dm
G7/B
C
F
G
bridge be - tween your heart and mine. ____
C
C/E
F
C/G
G7
Love can build a bridge, don't you think_ it's time? ____ Don't you think_ it's time? ____

Additional Lyrics

2. I would whisper love so loudly,
Every heart would understand
That love and only love can
Join the tribes of man.
I would give my heart's desires
So that you might see.
The first step is to realize
That it all begins with you and me. *(To Chorus)*

A Few Good Things Remain

Words and Music by
Pat Alger and Jon Vezner

C
D
G
A
Am7
Bm7
G/B
A/C#
And fear gave way to bet - ter things and sweet - er dreams.
When dust set - tles on my dreams, you wash them clean.
D7sus4
E7sus4
D7
E7
G
A
G/F#
A/G#
Em7
F#m7
G/D
A/E
Like a warm spring rain on the roof a -
3. Instrumental
Cadd2
Dadd2
G6/B
A6/C#
Am7
Bm7
D7sus4
E7sus4
D7
E7
G
A
G/F#
A/G#
bove, the way you call my name
Em7
F#m7
G/D
A/E
Cadd2
Dadd2
D
E
when we make love. While the world

Cmaj7
Dmaj7
D
E
Em
F#m
Bm7
C#m7
out - side — my win - dow goes — in - sane, —
Em
F#m
G/D
A/E
C add 2
Dadd2
D
To Coda
E
you're here to re - mind — me,
a few good things re - main. —
1. G
A
Em7
F#m7
G
A
Em7
F#m7
2. G
A
D.S. al Coda
C/D
D/E
3fr.
D
E

Coda
D
E
Em
F#m
C
D
C/B
D/C#
a few good things re-main.
You're here to re-
Am7
Bm7
D7sus4
E7sus4
mind me,
a few good things re-main.
G
A
Em7
F#m7
G
A
Em7
F#m7
Am7
Bm7
D7sus4
E7sus4
G
A
rit.

Deeper Than The Holler

Words and Music by
Paul Overstreet and Don Schlitz

but I've heard that o-cean's salt-y and the stars, some-times they
there's at least a mil-lion love songs that peo-ple love to

fall. And that would not do jus-tice to the way I feel for
sing. And ev-'ry one is dif-f'rent and ev-'ry-one's the

you, so I had to sing a song a-bout all the things I knew.
same and this is just an-oth-er way of say-ing the same thing.

My love is deep-er than the hol-ler,

strong-er than the riv-er, high-er than the pine trees grow-ing

Bb   C7   F   Bb
tall up-on_ the hill. My love is pur-er than the snow-flakes ___ that
F   Am/E   Dm   Gm 3fr.   F/A
fall in late_ De-cem-ber ___ and hon-est as _ a rob-in on_ the
Bb   Gm 3fr.   C7   To Coda
spring-time win-dow sill, ___ and long-er than_ the song of a whip-poor-will..
F   Dm   Gm 3fr.   C7   D.S. al Coda
From the
Coda F   Dm   Gm 3fr.   C7   F
rit.

Longer

Words and Music by
Dan Fogelberg

Moderate Ballad

high - er than___ an - y bird ev - er flew,___
tru - er than___ an - y tree ev - er grew,___
burn - ing lines___ in the book of our lives.___ Though the

Long - er than___ there've been stars up in the hea - vens,___
Deep - er than___ an - y for - est prim - e - val,___
bind - ing cracks___ and the pag - es start to___ yel-low,

I've been in love___ with you.___
I am in love___ with you.___
I'll be in love___ with you.

F(add9)/C   C   Eb(add9)/Bb   Bb
I'll bring fi - re in the win - ters;
F(add9)/C   C   Eb(add9)/Bb   Bb
you'll send show - ers in the springs.
F(add9)/C   C   Eb(add9)/Bb   Bb
We'll fly through the falls and sum - mers with
D7sus/G   D7/F#   Dm7/F   D7/F#
D.S. al Coda
love on our wings.
CODA   G   G/A

Bb   D7/A   G   F(add9)/C   C
I'll be in love with you.
Eb(add9)/Bb   Bb   F(add9)/C   C   Eb(add9)/Bb   Bb
F(add9)/C   C   Eb(add9)/Bb   Bb   D7sus/G   D7/F#   Dm7/F   D7/F#
G   Am7   Gmaj7/B   C
Long - er than   there've been fish - es   in the o - cean,

G Am7 Gmaj7/B C
high - er than an - y bird ev - er flew,
G Am7 Gmaj7/B C
Long - er than there've been stars up in the hea - vens,
Bb D7/A G G/A Bb D7/A
I've been in love with you, I am in love with you.
G G/A Bb D7/A G

Part Of Me

G   Am7   G/B   C
There's a part of me that wish-es
C7   F   C/E
all my dreams come true,
Dm   G   Dm7   C/E
and a part of me that prays that I'll wake up some-
F   G   C   To Coda   G   Am7   G/B
1.
day o-ver you.
I throw a pen-ny on the

2.
C 7
F
C/E
The way it comes   and
Dm
G
goes,
rid - in' high,
C
D.S. al Coda
fall - in' low.
There's a part of me that
Coda
C
G7
C
rit.

Annie's Song

A7
G
rain,
Like a storm in the des -
A
Bm
G
D
D/C#
ert,
like a sleep - y blue o - cean,
D/B
D/A
G
F#m
Em
You fill up my sens - es,
come
A7
D
Dsus4
D
Dsus4
fill me a - gain.
Come let me

G   A   Bm   G
love
sens   -   es   let   me   give   my   life
like   a   night   my   in   a

D   D/C#   D/B   D/A   G
to   you,
for   -   est,   Let   me   drown   in   your   laugh   -
Like   the   moun   -   tains   in   spring

F#m   Em   G   A7
ter,
time,   let   me   die   in   your   arms.
like   a   walk   in   the   rain.

G   A   Bm
Let   me   lay   down   be   -   side
Like   a   storm   in   the   des   you,   let   me
-    ert,   like   a

G   D   D/C#   D/B   D/A
al - ways be with you, You Come let me
sleep - y blue o - cean, fill up my
G   F#m   Em   A7   1. D
love you come love me a - gain
sesns - es, come fill me a -
Dsus4   D   Dsus4   2. D   Dsus4
You fill up my gain.
dim.
D   Dsus4   D   Dsus4   D

Love Is Strong

F
Fsus2/A
B♭
It takes a lot just to stand there,
with your ten - der ways you wooed me,
you
Am7
B♭add2 3fr.
Am7
B♭add2 3fr.
C7sus4
choos-ing to be meek, ap - pear-ing to be weak.
turned my life a-round, you
But love is
Play 1st time only
Play 2nd time only
Am7
B♭add2 3fr.
C7sus4
C7
bare - ly made a sound.
Love is
F
F/A
B♭
C
strong, love is stro ong.
mf, f
F
Dm7
G7sus4
G7
C7sus4
C7
It can move a moun - tain, it can roll a - way the stone.
Love is

F   Fsus2/A F/A   B♭   G7/B   F/C   A/C♯
To Coda
strong,   love is stro - ong,   but nev - er de - mands   its own
Dm   B♭   F/C   C7sus4   1. F   F/A
way.   No,   love nev - er de - mands   its own   way.
L.H. (melody)
B♭   F   F/A   B♭
2. F   C7sus4   C7   F/C
way.   It's nev - er hope - less   for the help - less.   (Help - less.)
C7sus4   C7   F/C
I was as help - less   as could be.   (Help - less.)

Am7
Bb
Now I've be-come a true be-liev - er,
Gm7
C7sus4
C7
D.S. al Coda
and it's a pow - er - ful thing. Love is
Dm
Bb
F/C
C7sus4
C7
Coda
way. No, love nev-er de-mands its own
dim.
F
F/A
Bb
L.H.
(melody)
mf way.
F
F/A
Bb
C7sus4
F
rit.

Love Chooses You

Words and Music by
Laurie Lewis

E
A
down to your shoes. It knows heart-ache and
E/G#
F#m
trial but ac-cepts no de - ni - al.
D
E
A
You can't choose who you love, love choos - es you.
1.
E
2.
2. In the
D/E
A
Tell me now if I'm wrong.

Chorus
D
E
Are you feel-in' the same?
A
D/A
A
Are your feet on the
D
E
E7
ground? Are you call-ing my
A
name?
Do you lie a-wake nights?
D
E
Please say you do.
42

A
'Cause you can't choose
Bm
D
E
who you love,
love choos -
A
D/A
To Coda
A
es you.
Bm
D
straight ♪'s
E
A
D/A
A
E7sus4
D.S. (with repeat)
al Coda
3. Love

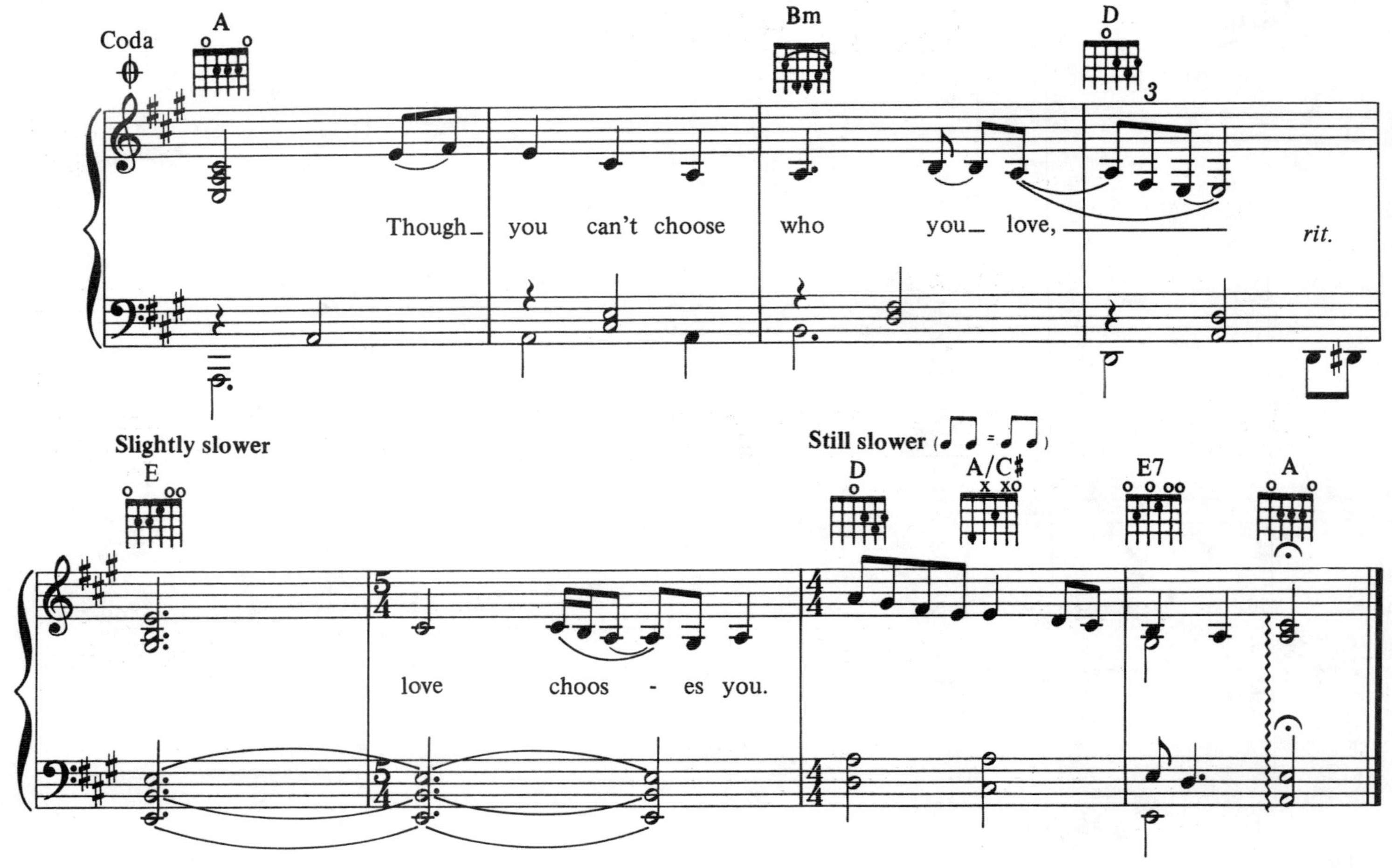

Additional Lyrics

2. In the wink of an eye love looses an arrow.
   We control it no more than the flight of the sparrow,
   The swell of the tide or the light of the moon.
   You can't choose who you love, love chooses you. *(To Chorus)*

3. Love cuts like a torch to a heart behind steel,
   And though you may hide it, love knows how you feel.
   And though you may trespass on the laws of the land,
   Your heart has to follow when love takes your hand.

4. And it seems we're two people within the same circle;
   It's drawn tighter and tighter till you're all that I see.
   I'm full and I'm empty and you're pouring through me
   Like a warm rain fallin' through the leaves on a tree. *(To Chorus)*

She Is His Only Need

Words and Music by
Dave Loggins

G
Am7
He nev-er had a lot of luck with the la-dies, but he sure had a lot of good work-ing skills.
D7
G
C/D
Nev-er cared a-bout climb-ing an-y lad-der.__ He knew the way in a small ca-fé.__ Found__
D
D7
G
__ the will:__ he met Miss Bon-nie and a lit-tle bit of her was a lit-tle too much.__
Em7
Am
G/B
Cmaj7
A few mov-ies and a few months lat - er __ the feel-ing got strong e-nough.__

D   G Gmaj7 C
He did-n't own a car so it must have been love: ___
D   D7 G   C/D
That drove him up-town for a dia - mond.___ That's when he start-ed goin'_
G   Am7
_ o-ver_ the line. _________ Work-ing o-ver-time _________
D7   G   C/D
to give her things just to hear her say she don't_ de-serve_ 'em. But he loved her and he just kept

G
Am7
go-in' o-ver-board, over the lim-it to af-ford
D7
G
Gmaj7
8va
to give her things he knew she want-ed. 'Cause with-out her where
Am7
D7
would he be? See, it's not for him.
loco
G
C/D
To Coda
G
She is his on-ly need.

C/D G
Ring on her fin-ger and one __ on the lad - der. __
Am7 D
A new pro-mo-tion ev-'ry now and then. __ Bon-nie worked un - til she could-n't tie her ap-ron, then
G C/D G Gmaj7
stayed at home and had the first of two chil - dren. And my, how the time ____ did fly!
Am7 D7
The ba- bies grew up and moved __ a - way. ____ Left 'em sit-ting on the front porch rock-ing __ and

G   C/D   D   D7
Bil- ly watch-ing Bon-nie's hair___ turn gray.   And ev- 'ry once in a while you could

G   Em7   Am   G/B
see him get up__ and he'd_ head_ down - town   'cause he'd heard a-bout some-thing she'd want - ed_

Cmaj7   D
__ and it just had_ to be found. _   Did-n't mat-ter how sim - ple or how much. It was

G   Gmaj7   C   D   D7
love. ______________   And boy, ain't that love just some - thing

G
C/D
D.S. al Coda
CODA
G
when it's strong e - nough to keep a man go - in'
need.
(O - ver the line, ____
(Instrumental on repeat)
Am7
D7
work-ing o - ver - time. ___
She is ___ his on - ly
His on - ly ___
G
C/D
G
Am7
need.
need.)
(O - ver-board, ___
o - ver the lim-it.
Just for her. _
D7
G
C/D
Repeat and Fade
His on - ly ___ need.
She is ___ his on - ly
need.)

The Battle Hymn Of Love

Words and Music by
Paul Overstreet and Don Schlitz

I'll for - sake my rest____ for your hap - pi - ness;____
till my death I will stand by____ you.____
E   A
Chorus
D
With God as my wit - ness____ this vow I will____
A
make,____ to have and to hold____ you, no oth - er to take.____

E
A
For rich or for poor, un-der skies gray or blue,
D
A
E
To Coda
1. A
till my death I will stand by you.
2. A
D.S. (lyric 1) al Coda
2. There are you. With
Coda
A
you. Till the bat - tle is won I

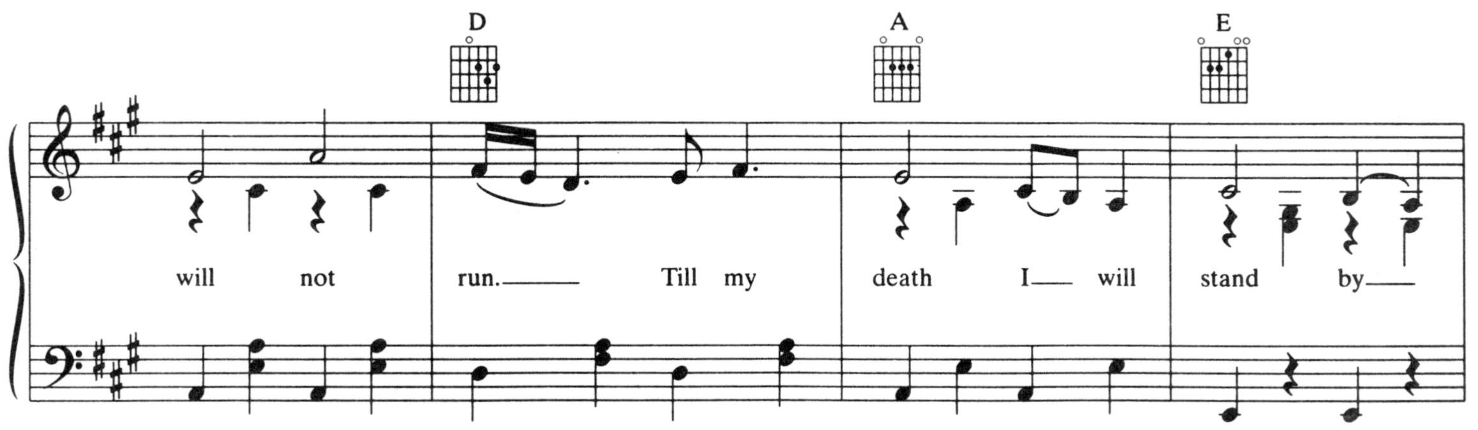

Additional Lyrics

2. There are wars and there are rumors,
   The wars yet to come.
   Temptations we'll have to walk through.
   Though others may tremble
   I will not run.
   Till my death I will stand by you.

2nd Chorus:
   I will put on the armor of faithfulness
   To fight for a heart that is true.
   Till the battle is won
   I will not rest.
   Till my death I will stand by you.

The Calm At The Center Of My Storm

E
F
D#m7b5
Em7b5
can see.
Cap - tured by the wind
A / E
Bb / F
that breaks so help - less - ly,
F#m7add4
Gm7add4
A sus2/ E
Bb sus2/F
B 7sus4
C7sus4
know if not for you there'd be no hope for me.
B7
C7
Chorus
E
F
A
Bb
You are the calm at the cen - ter of my storm.

E
F
When the cold winds blow,
C#m / Dm
B/D# / C/E
A / Bb
you're the fire that keeps me warm.
When this
E / F
A / Bb
E / F
B/D# / C/E
old world gets me down,
I will rest in - side your arms.
A / Bb
E/G# / F/A
F#m7add4 / Gm7add4
B7sus4 / C7sus4
You are the calm at the cen - ter of my storm.

2. If I could only learn to always turn to you,
Instead of thinking I always know what to do...
Why does it take the darkness for my eyes to see?
There's never been a time when you weren't there for me. *(To Chorus)*

'Til The Mountains Disappear

A
E
I've placed a gold - en ring up - on your hand.
like the heart of a fair weath - er friend.

B7
Now my heart is tell - ing me
But if ev - er for one mo -

E
I should be bold - er, and
ment you should doubt me, well,

A
E
F#m
G#m
take you to the high - est place that you have ev - er been
I will just start climb - ing through the snow and through the wind

A   F#m   G#m   A   B
and   say   it   all   a - gain: I'll   pledge   my
to   say   it   all   a - gain:

A   E
love   to   you   on   top   of   a   moun-

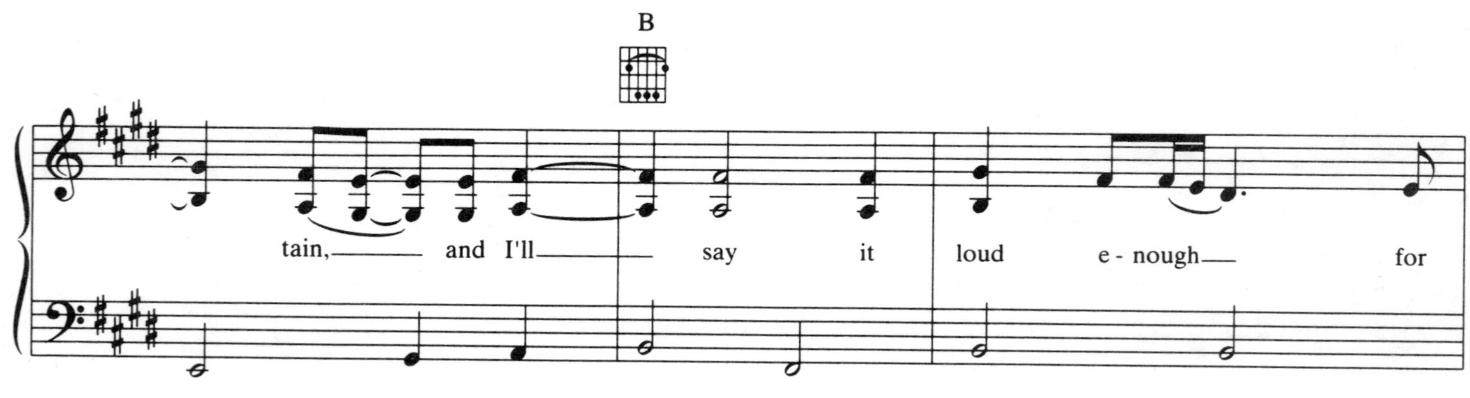

B
tain,   and   I'll   say   it   loud   e - nough   for

E   E7   A
all   the   world   to   hear.   We'll   let   it   ech - o   through

E
the deep - est, dark - est can - yon, and I'll
B
be your com-pan - ion 'til the moun - tains dis - ap - pear.
E
To Coda
1.
2.
D.S. al Coda
I'll pledge my
Coda
B
Yes, I will be your com-pan - ion 'til the moun-
E
tains dis - ap - pear.

Unanswered Prayers

Words and Music by
Pat Alger, Garth Brooks
and Larry Bastian

Em   D/F#   G   Asus4   A
n't help but think of the way things used to be.
Em7   D/F#   Asus4
er ask for an-y-thing a-gain.
Chorus
A   D   F#m7
Some-times I thank God for un-
G   Asus4   D   A/C#   Bm   D/A
an-swered prayers. Re-mem-ber when you're talk-in' to the
Em7   A   D   D7
man up-stairs, just be-cause he does-n't an-swer does-n't

G
E7
D
Bm
mean he don't care. Some of God's great-est gifts ____
Em
A
D
D/F#
are un - an - swered pray - ers. ____
G
Asus4
A
D.S. al Coda
3. She
Coda
Em7
D/F#
Asus4
Lord knows ____ what he's do - in' af - ter ____ all. ____
A
F#m
G
And as she walked ____ a - way ____ I

F#m   Bm   Em7   D/F#
looked at my wife, ___ and then and there I thanked the good ___ Lord for the

G   Asus4   A
gifts in my ___ life. ___ Some - times I thank ___

D   F#m7   G   Asus4
God ___ for un - an - swered prayers. ___ Re -

D   A/C#   Bm   D/A   Em7   A
mem - ber when you're talk - in' to the man up - stairs, ___ just be - cause ___

D   D7   G   E7
___ he does - n't an - swer does - n't mean he don't care. ___ Some of

Additional Lyrics

2. She was the one that I wanted for all times,
   And each night I'd spend prayin' that God would make her mine.
   And if you'd only grant me this wish I wished back then,
   I'd never ask for anything again. *(To Chorus)*

3. She wasn't quite the angel
   That I remembered in my dreams,
   And I could tell the time changed me,
   In her eyes too it seemed.
   We tried to talk about the old days.
   Wasn't much we could recall.
   I guess the Lord knows what he's doin' after all. *etc.*

Lines Around Your Eyes

Words and Music by
Lucinda Williams

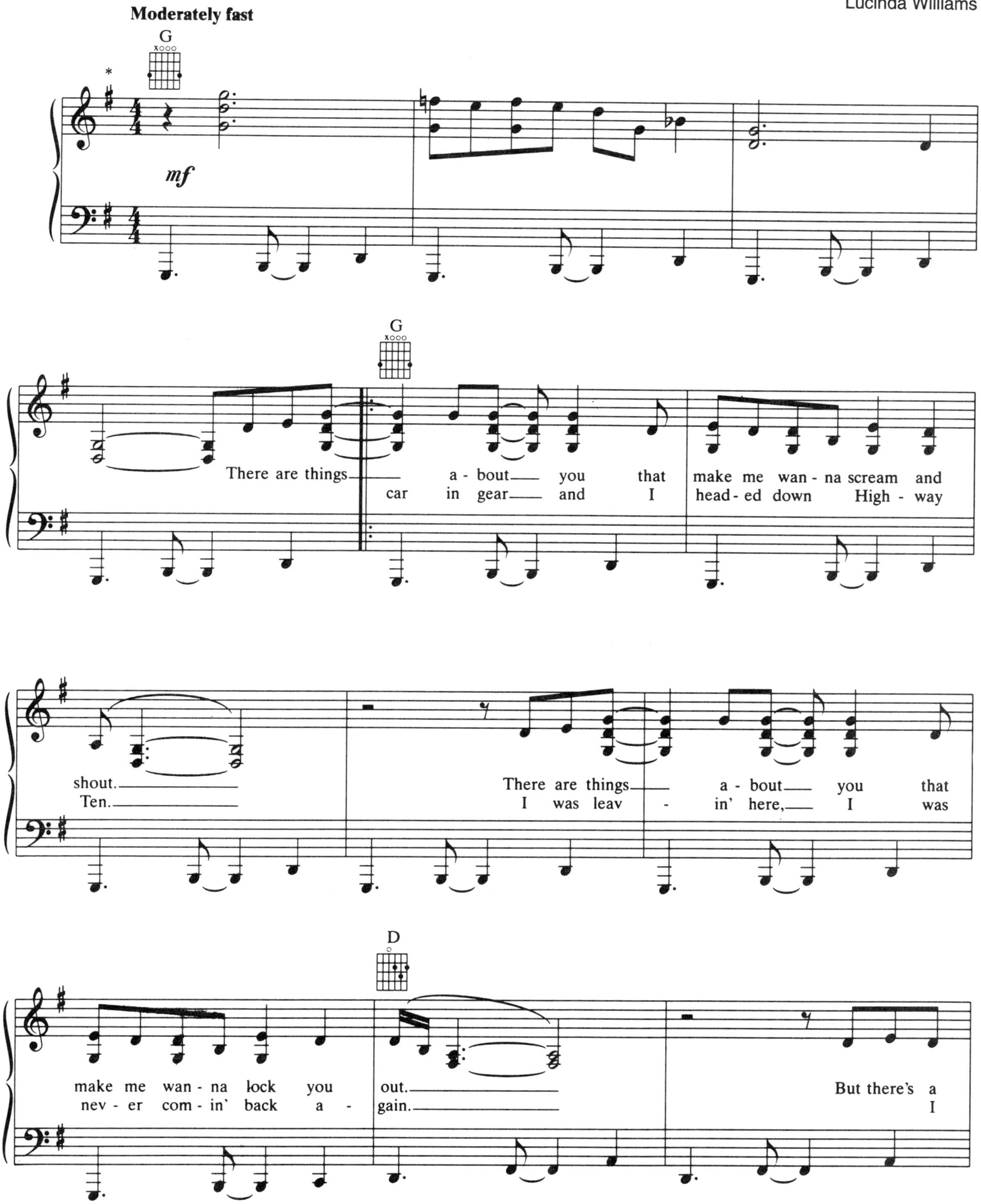

* Recorded a half step lower.

G
lit - tle thing___ that drives me___ wild,___ some-thing that hap - pens ev - 'ry
got a-bout as far as the Tex - as___ line.___ I still could-n't get___ you
D
time you smile.___ I can't get o - ver the lines___ a - round your
off of my mind.___ 'Cause I can't get o - ver the lines___ a - round your
G
eyes.___
eyes.___
D
Lines a - round you eyes___
G
___ ev - 'ry time you___ smile.___ And the way___
D
___ you touch___ me, dar - lin', just drives me___ wild.___
G

D
Some - times I don't know what we're fight - in' a - bout,___ but
C
G
that don't mean___ we can't work things out. 'Cause I love you, dar - lin', and the
D
G
1.
lines___ a - round your eyes.___ I put my
2.
'Cause I love___ you, dar - lin', and the
D
G
lines___ a - round your eyes.

Like I Used To Do

Words and Music by
Pat Alger and Tim O'Brien

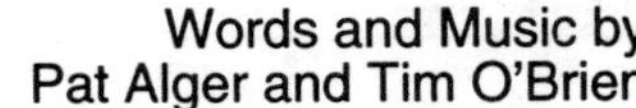

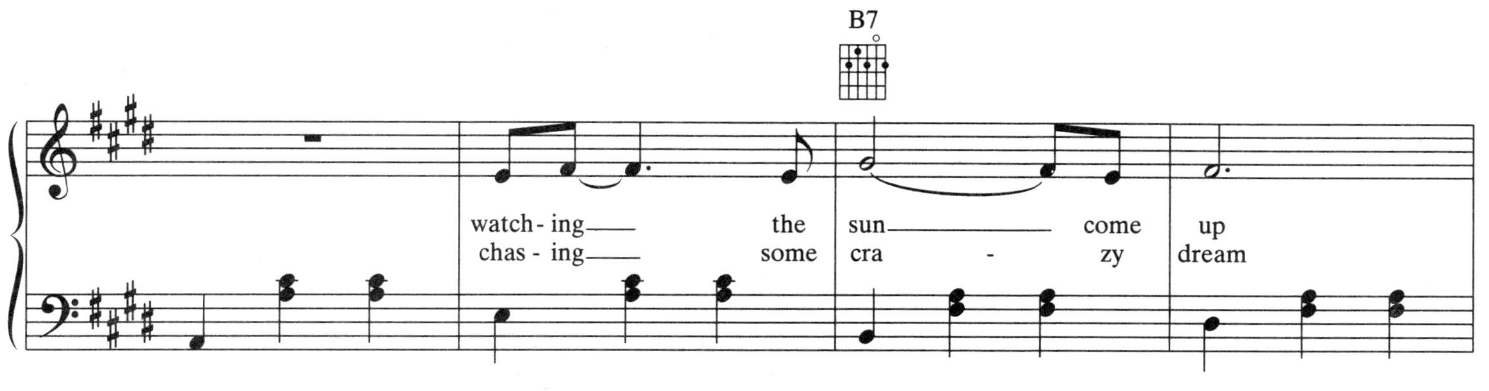

B7
watch - ing the sun come up
chas - ing some cra - zy dream

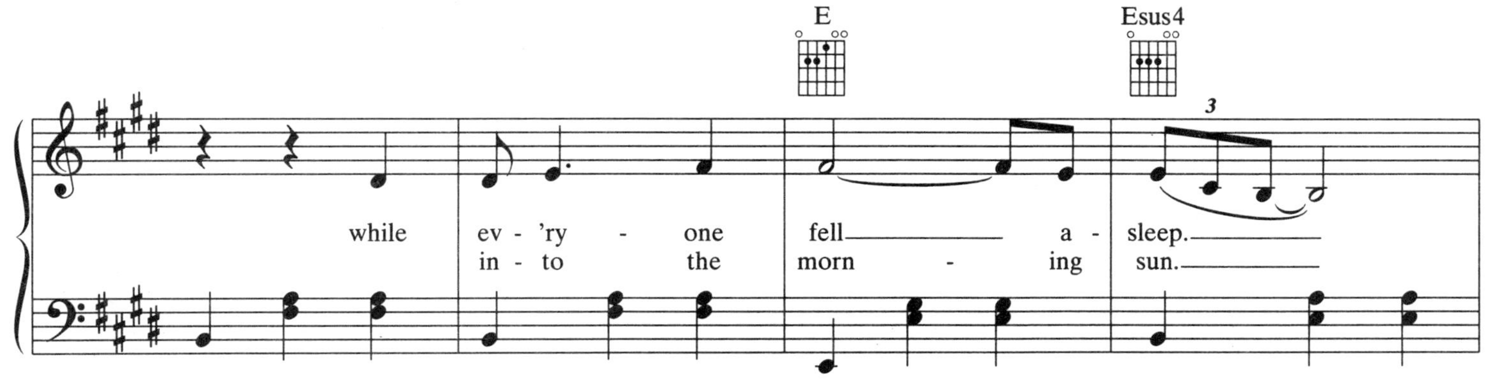

E
Esus4
while ev - 'ry - one fell a - sleep.
in - to the morn - ing sun.

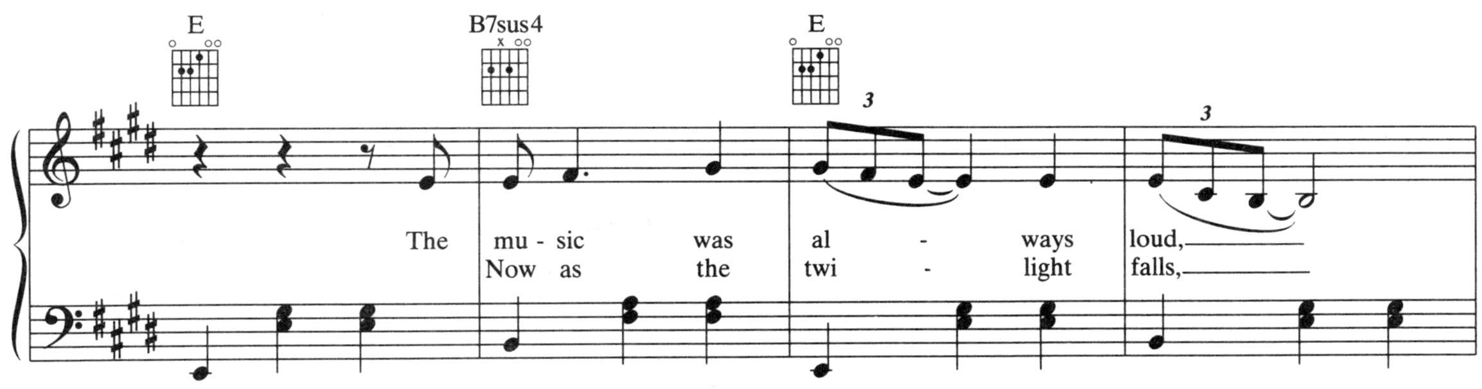

E
B7sus4
E
The mu - sic was al - ways loud,
Now as was the twi - light falls,

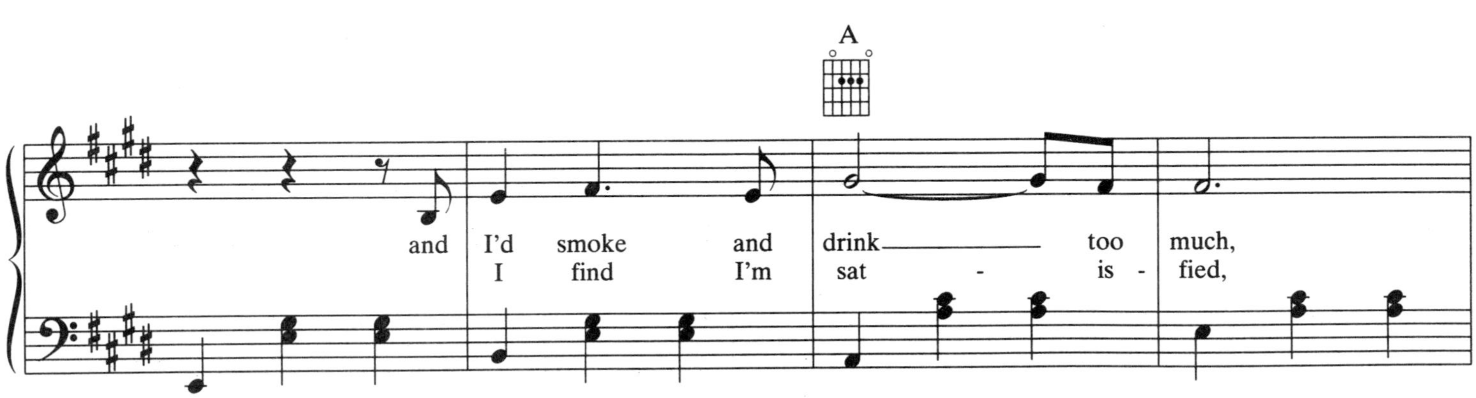

A
and I'd smoke and drink too much,
I find I'm sat - is - fied,

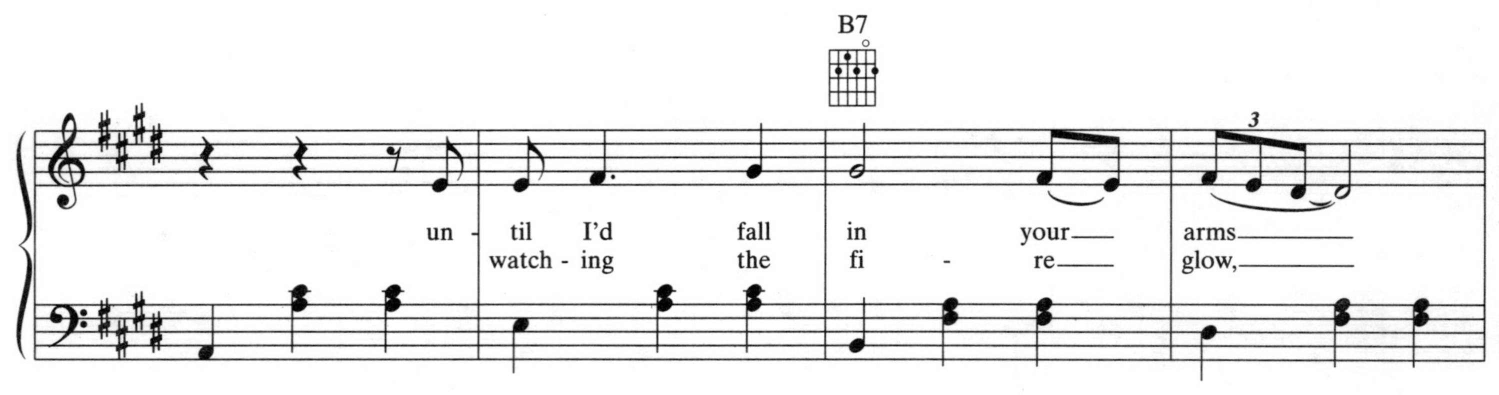

B7
un - til I'd fall in your____ arms____
watch - ing the fi - re____ glow,____

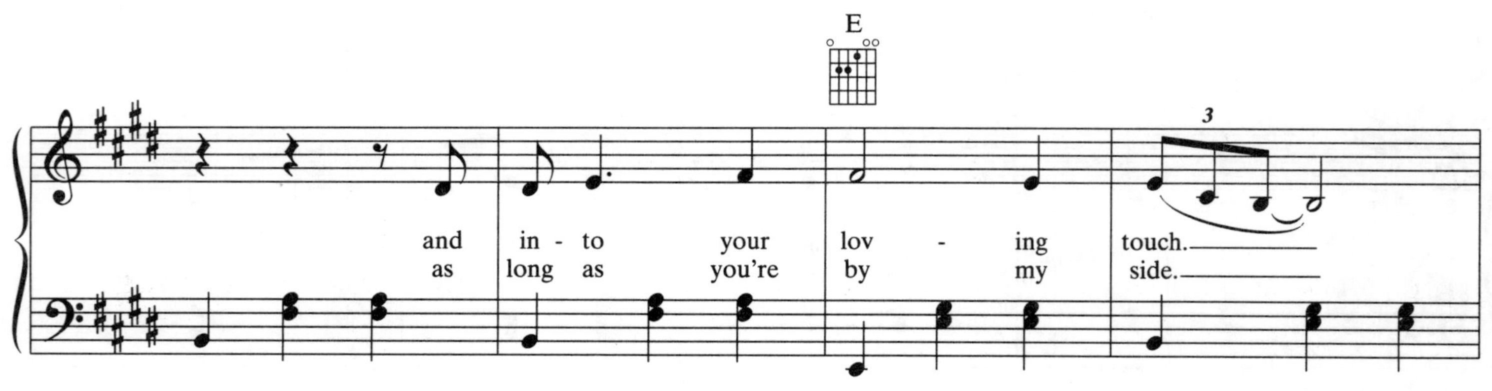

E
and in - to your lov - ing touch.____
as long as you're by my side.____

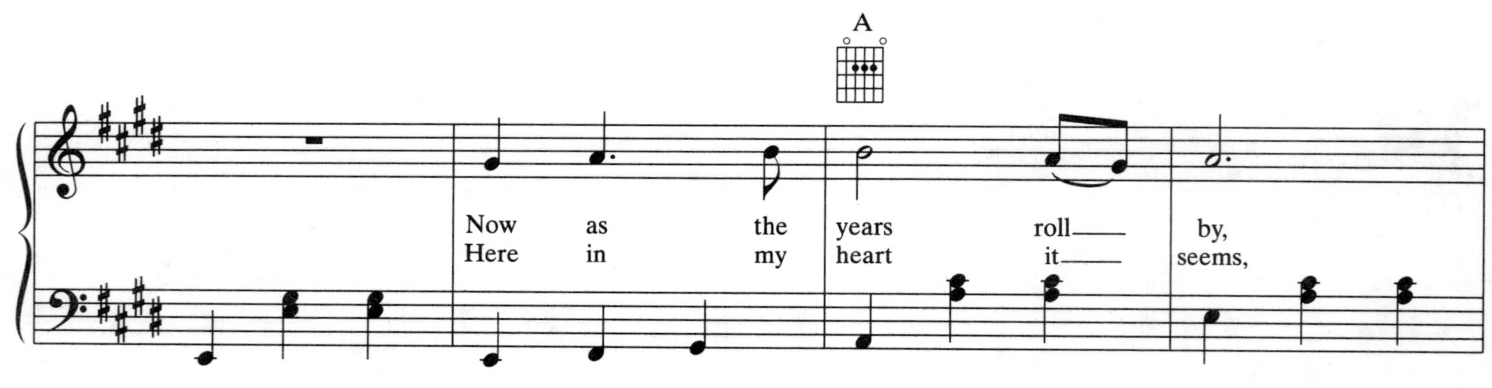

A
Now as the years roll____ by,
Here in my heart it____ seems,

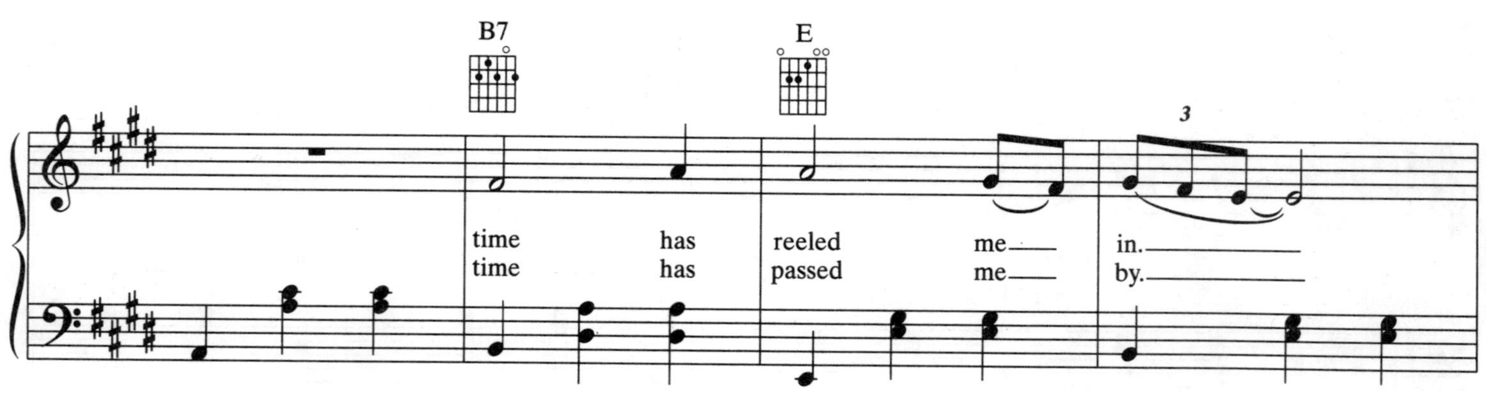

B7   E
time has reeled me____ in.____
time has passed me____ by.____

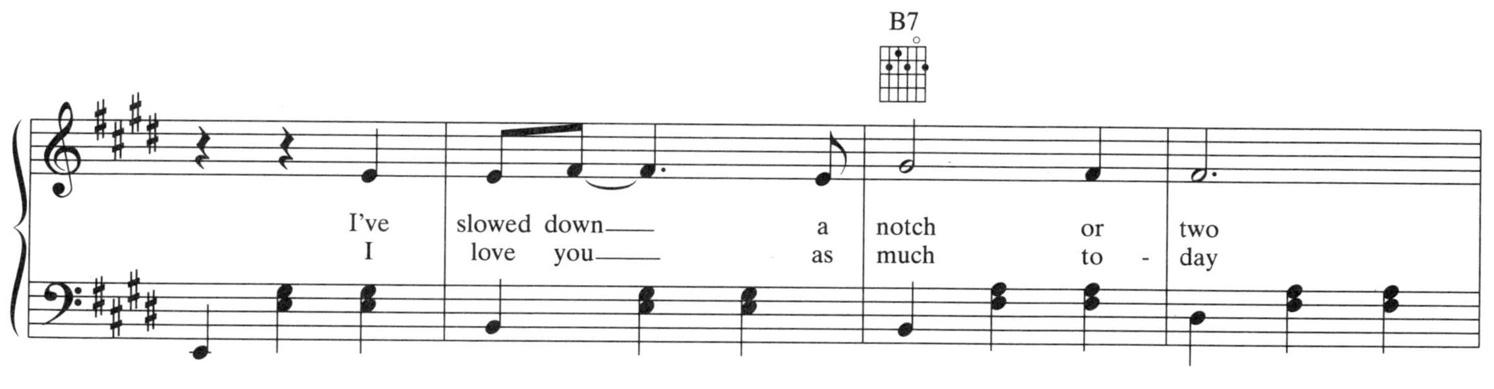

B7
I've slowed down a notch or two
I love you as much to - day

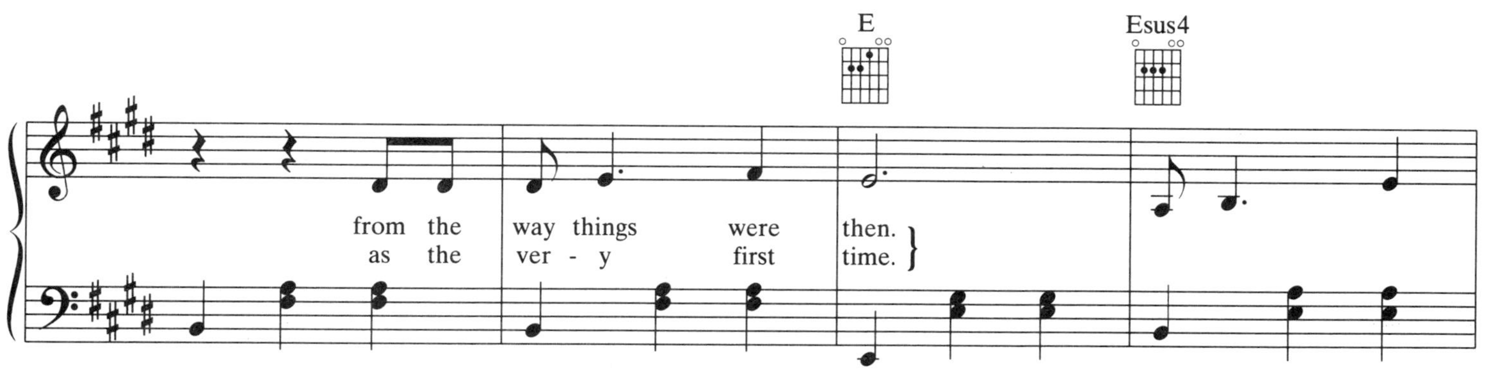

E   Esus4
from the way things were then.
as the ver - y first time.

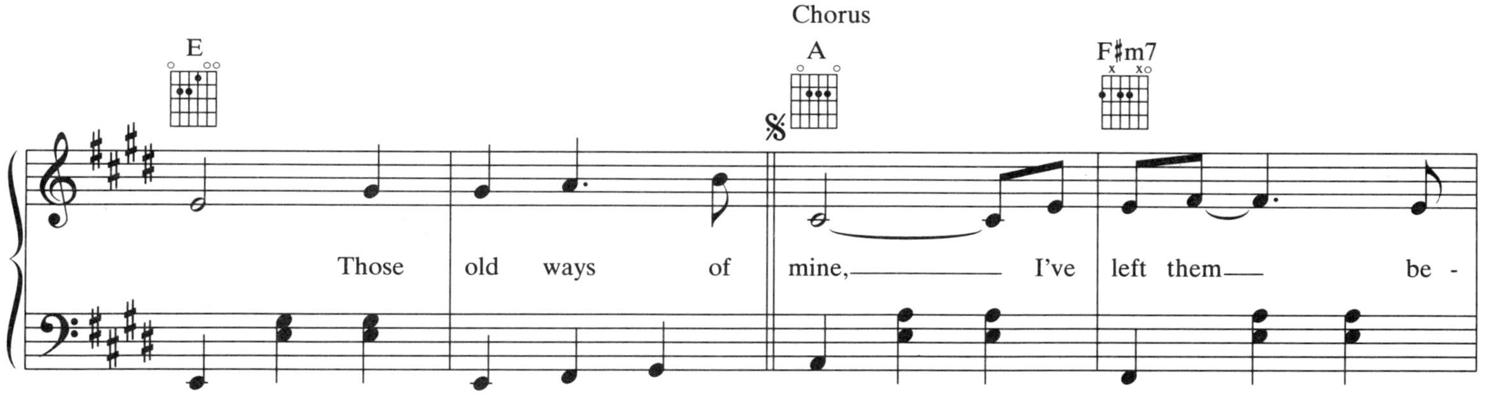

E   Chorus   A   F#m7
Those old ways of mine, I've left them be -

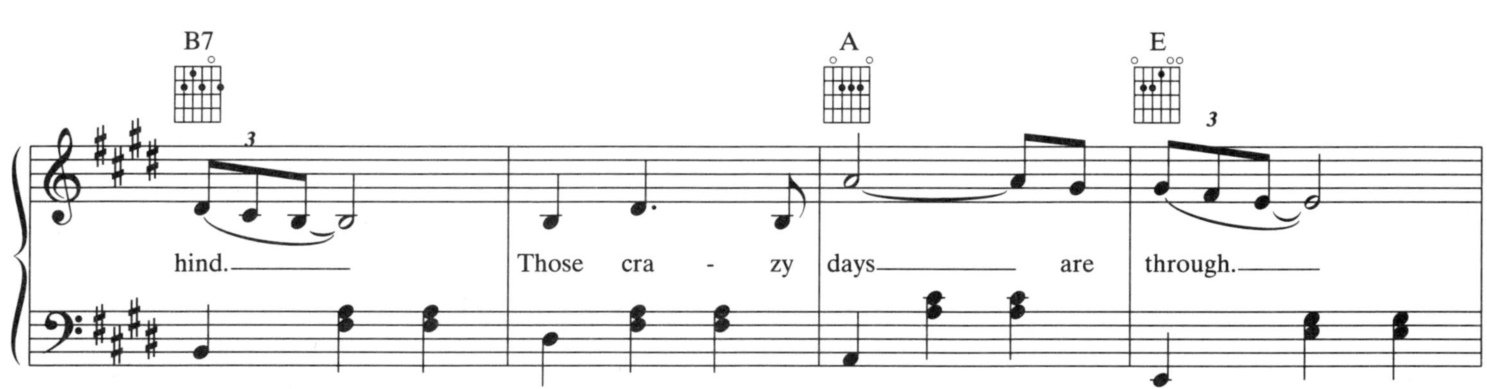

B7   A   E
hind. Those cra - zy days are through.

A
F#m7
The on-ly thing I still do like I used to
B7
A
E
To Coda
1.
do is car-ry this torch for you.
Esus4
E
B7
E
2.
2. Re-mem-ber the you.
A
I still want you the way I want-ed you
E
B7sus4
E
then.
If I could

B7
do it all o - ver, I'd do it all o - ver a -
E   Esus4   E
D.S. al Coda
gain. Those old ways of
Coda   E   A
you. The on - ly thing I still do like
B7   A
I used to do is car - ry this torch
E   Esus4   E
for you.
rit.
77

Lady

*Recorded 1/2 step higher

78

Gm/D
C/D
Dm
To Coda
hold you in my arms for - ev - er more.
hear you whis - per soft - ly in my ear.
You have
In my
Gm7
Am7
D
Bbmaj7
Am7
gone and made me such a fool,
I'm so lost in your
mf
Dsus
D
Gm7
Am7
D7
love.
And oh, we be - long to - geth - er,
Bbmaj7
Am7
Dsus
D
D.S. al Coda
Won't you be - lieve in my song?

Gm7
Am7
D7
B♭maj7
Am7
Coda
mf
eyes _____ I see no _____ one else but you, There's no _____ oth - er love like
Dsus
D
Gm7
Am7
D7
our love. _____ And yes, _____ oh yes, I'll al - ways want you near me,
B♭maj7
Am7
Dsus
D
B♭
3
I've wait - ed for you _____ for so long. _____ La - dy, _____
f
C/B♭
F
C/E
Dm
Dm/C
B♭
your love's the on - ly love I need, And be - side me

C/Bb   F   C/E   Dm   Dm/C
is where   I want you   to be.____   'Cause
Bb   C/Bb   F   C/E
my love,____   there's some-thing   I____   want you____   to
Dm   Dm/C   Bb   Gm7 3fr.   C11
know.   You're the love____   of my life,____   you're my
Dm   Gm/D   C/D   Dm
La-dy.____   Slower   8va
mp

I'll Leave This World Loving You

Words and Music by
Wayne Kemp

C   F
hear _____________ from ___ you. _____   If we
they'll ____________ see me through. ____   If we

F7   Bb
nev - er meet a - gain _______   be - fore ___ my _____ life   is
nev - er meet a - gain _______   I'll love _____ you   for -

F
o - ver,   I'll   leave _________   this
ev - er.   I'll   leave _________________ this ___

C7
F
1
world lov - ing you.
world lov - ing you.
You can
2
Bb
You were mine for a time and I'm
F
thank - ful. _
Oh, but life would be so

C
lone - some _ with - out ___ you. ___
If we
F
nev - er meet a - gain ___________ this side of
Bb
hea - ven, _____________
F
I'll leave _________ this ___

C
F
B♭
world   lov - ing   you. ________
F
C
F
D♭
G♭
If   we   nev -   er   meet   a -

Gb/Bb
Cb
gain ________ this side of hea - ven, ________
Gb
Db
I'll leave ________ this ___ world lov - ing
Cb
Gb/Bb   Abm   Gb
you. ________

I Won't Take Less Than Your Love

Words and Music by
Paul Overstreet and Don Schlitz

dia - monds?   Shall I   buy___   you   furs?_______________
tem - ple?   Shall I   make a   sac - ri - fice?_______________

Bb   C   Bb
Say_____________   the word_______   and it's   yours."____
Tell   me Lord,_   and I ___   will pay the   price."____

C   F
And his wife said,} "I   won't   take   less   than your   love,   sweet
And the Lord said,}

Bb   F
love.___ No, I   won't   take   less   than your   love.___

All the {rich - es / treas - ures} of the world________ could
nev- er be e -nough,________ and I won't take less than your love."
Dm   Bb   C
To Coda
F   C
C
"How much do I owe,________ you," to the
F
moth- er said the son,________ "for all that you_ have taught me in the

C
days when I was young? Shall I bring ex-pen-sive blan-
C7
kets to cast up-on your bed, and a
F   G   F   G
pil-low for to rest your wea-ry head?" And the moth-er said, "I
C
won't take less than your love, sweet love. No, I
F   C
won't take less than your love. All the

Am
com - forts of the world _____ could nev - er be e - nough, _____ and I
F   G   C
won't _ take less than your love." _
Am   G   F
Am   G   F
D.S. al Coda
Coda   Bb   C   F
won't take less ... I won't take less than your

Bb
love, sweet love.__ No, I won't take less than your
F
love.__ All the treas - ures of__ the world__ could
Dm   Bb   C
nev - er be e - nough.__ And I won't __ take less than your
F   Bb   C
love. No, I won't__ take less than your
F
love"__

Forever And Ever, Amen

Words and Music by
Paul Overstreet and Don Schlitz

2.
A7
Chorus
D
un - til the day that I die.
cresc.
I'm gon - na love
f
G
D
G
you for - ev - er, for - ev - er and al -
D
G
ways, a - men. As long as old men
D
E7
sit and talk a - bout the weath - er, as long as old wom -
A7
D
en sit and talk a - bout old men. If you won - der how long

G
D
G
I'll be faith - ful, ____ I'll be hap - py to tell ____
just lis - ten to how ____
E7
G
you a - gain. ____ I'm gon - na love ____
this song ends. ____
A
D
G
E7
you for - ev - er and ev - er, for - ev - er and ev -
A
D
To Coda
D.S. (with repeat) al Coda
er, ____ a - men.
dim.
3. They say
Coda
G
A
D
I'm gon - na love ____ you for - ev - er and ev -

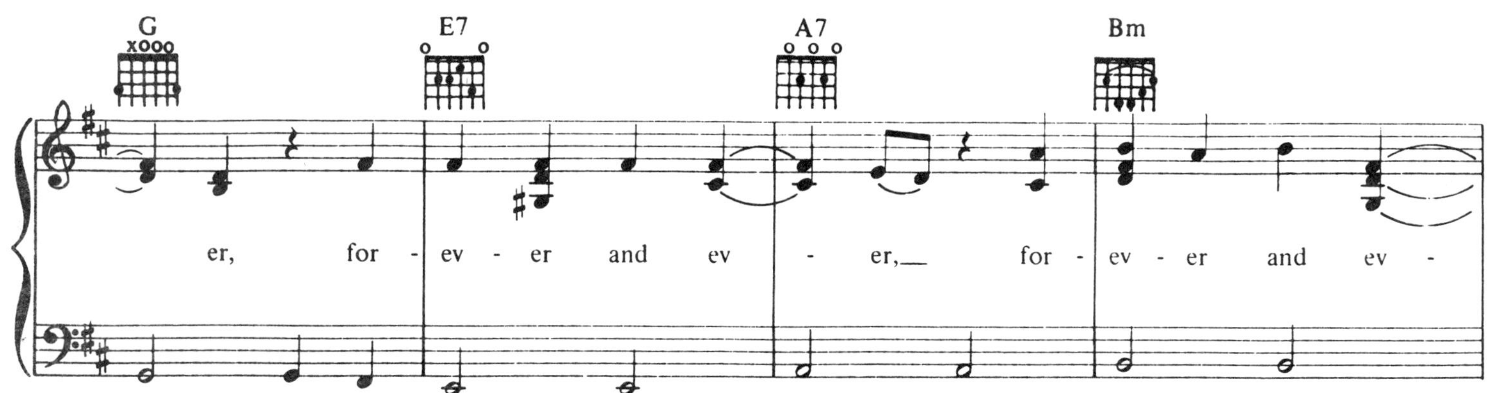

Additional Lyrics

2. You're not just time that I'm killing.
   I'm no longer one of those guys.
   As sure as I live, this love that I give
   Is gonna be yours until the day that I die. *(To Chorus)*

3. They say time takes its toll on a body,
   Makes a young girl's brown hair turn gray.
   Well honey, I don't care. I ain't in love with your hair.
   And if it all fell out I'd love you anyway.

4. Well, they say time can play tricks on a memory,
   Make people forget things they knew.
   Well, it's easy to see it's happening to me.
   I've already forgotten every woman but you. *(To Chorus)*

Goin' Gone

A
no one to re - turn____ to____
1.
F#m7
B7sus4 2fr.
as I wan - dered through the night.

2.
F#m7
B7sus4 2fr.
and I would look__ for love__ no more.____
cresc.
Chorus
A
E
Deep in the wa - ters__ of__ love I am
mf

fall - in' ___ sink - ing like a stone. ___

Deep in my ___

heart I ___ can ___ hear ___ love call - in'. ___ Go - in' once, ___

go - in' twice, ___ go - in' gone; ___

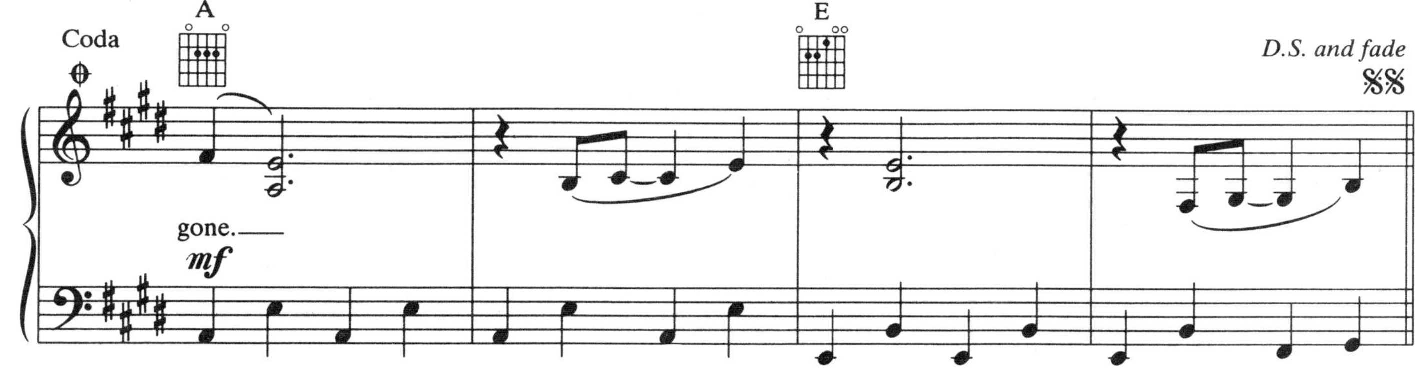

Additional Lyrics

2. From the first time that I saw you
Standing silent by the shore,
I knew my search was over,
And I would look for love no more. *(To Chorus)*

3. There's a ship on the horizon
Makin' its way against the wind.
Fom the place where I stand watchin',
I swear my ship is comin' in. *(To Chorus)*

I Know Where Love Lives

1.
2.
Chorus
E A E A D
— Mon - ser - rat. — love en - joys. I— know— where love—
A Bm D F#m
— lives. I know— where love— lives.
D E A
She's sit - ting on the back step in the eve - ning air,—
D E A
with sea - green eyes— and her chest - nut hair.—

Bm
D
F#m
To Coda
D
You keep your man - sions of gold, bud-dy, I don't care. 'Cause I
A
D
know where love lives.
E
A
D
E
A
Bm
D
F#m
D

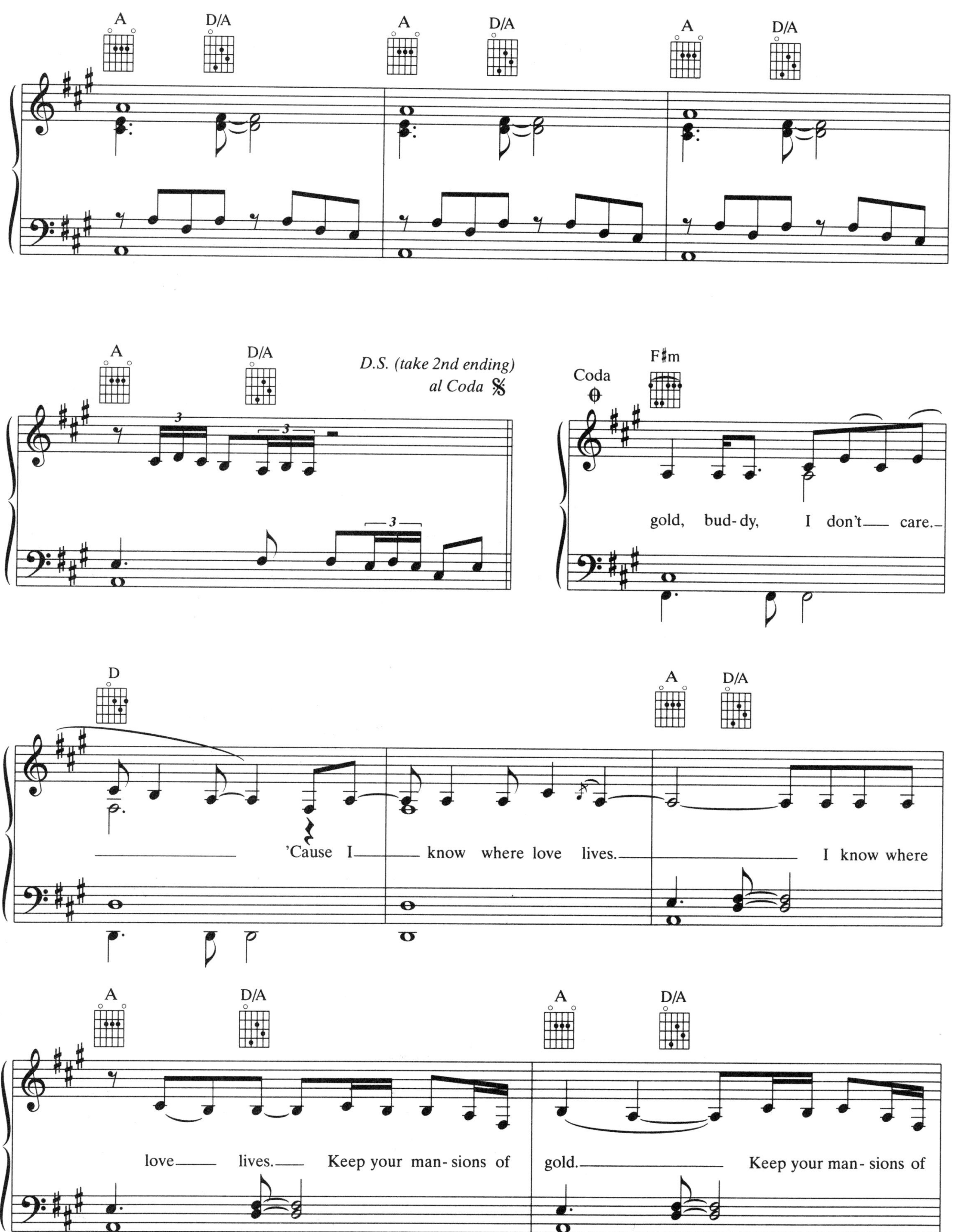

A
D/A
A
D/A
A
D/A
A
D/A
D.S. (take 2nd ending)
al Coda
Coda
F#m
gold, bud-dy, I don't care.
D
A
D/A
'Cause I know where love lives.
I know where
A
D/A
A
D/A
love lives. Keep your man-sions of
gold. Keep your man-sions of

Additional Lyrics

2. There's a house on the edge of town.
   It's a little old, it's a little run down.
   Full of laughter and tears and toys,
   Crazy things only love enjoys. *(To Chorus)*

3. You keep all that your fortune brings,
   All your fancy words, all your precious things.
   No matter what all your money buys,
   It's in the arms of love that true treasure lies. *(To Chorus)*

106

This Shirt

I've had it now for more ___ damn years ___ than I ___
where I used to set ___ my heart ___ up right ___

___ could count ___ an-y-way.
___ there where an-y-one ___ could see.

I wear it be-neath ___
This shirt is the

___ my jack-et with the col-lar turned ___
one I wore ___ to ev-'ry bor-ing high ___

___ up high. ___
___ school dance where the boys ig-nored ___ the girls and we

So old I should ___ re-place it,

Bb   C   F
but I'm not a-bout to try.
all pre-tend-ed to like the band.
F/Bb   F   F/E
Am   Bb
This shirt was a pil-low for my head
This shirt was the place your cat de-cid-
F   C   Am
on a train through It-a-ly.
-ed to give birth to five.
This shirt was a
And we stayed up all

Bb   F
blan - ket be - neath   the   love ___   we   made ___ in   Ar -
___ night watch - ing   and   we wept   when the

C   Am   Bb
 - ge - les. ___   This shirt was   lost for three ___ whole days ___
last ___ ge - les. one ___ died.   This shirt is   just   an   old ___   fad -

F   C   Dm
___ in a town ___   near Buf - fa - lo   till I ___ found the
 - ed piece of cot - ton   shin - ing like the

F/C   G/B
lock - er key   in a   down - town   Trail -
mem - o - ries   in - side

C   F   F/Bb
- ways   bus __   de - pot. ___
those   sil - ver   but - tons.

F   F/E   F

F/Bb   F   F/E

F   Bb/F   F
This   shirt   is   the   one   I   lent __ you.   And __ when __ you   gave __
This   shirt   is   a   grand   old   rel - ic   with   a   grand _ old

C
it back, __ it had a rip in - side __
his - to - ry. ____ I wear it now for Sun -

Bb/F   F   C
__ the sleeve __ where you rolled your __ cig - a - rettes.
- day chores, __ clean - ing house and rak - ing leaves. __

Dm   Dm/C   Bb
It was the place I put __ my heart, __ now look at where __ you've put
I wear it be - neath __ my jack - et with the col - lar turned __

C   Dm   Dm/C
a tear.
__ up high.   So old I should re - place it, __
I for - gave your thought - less - ness __ but

Bb
To Coda
C
D.S. al Coda
not the boy who put it there
but I'm
CODA
C
F
not a - bout to try.
Bb/F
F
C/F
F
Bb/F
F
C/F
Repeat and Fade
113

I Should Be With You

Words and Music by
Steve Wariner and Don Schlitz

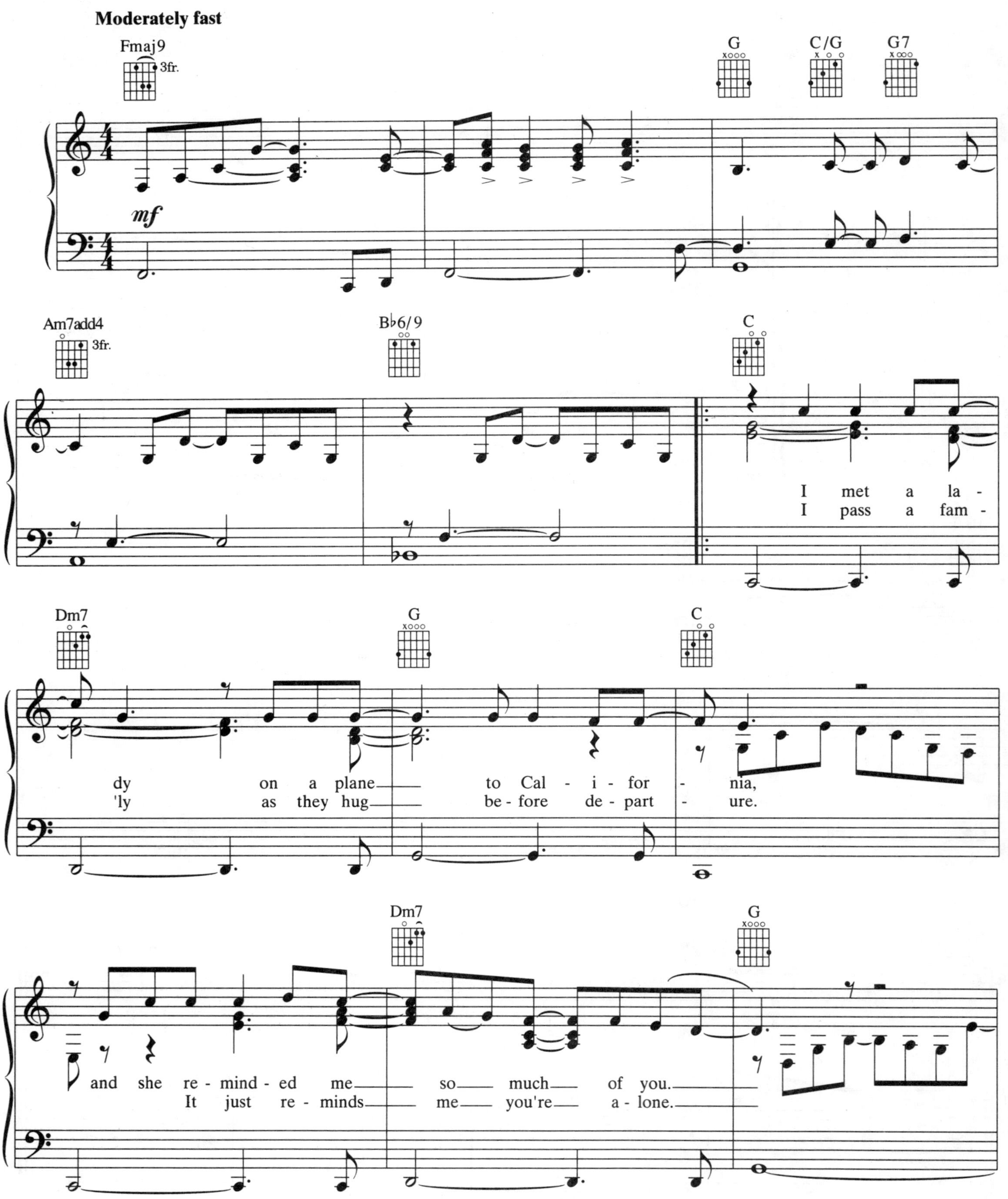

114

C
Dm7
When she asked what I___ was___ do - ing here,
I hold the quar - ter___ that will

G
Am7add4
3fr.
Bb6/9
well, then it hit me,
take my voice back to you
the cra - zy things the dol -
and hear you say I need___

F/A
G7
C
lar makes___ us do.___
you here___ at home.
I should be___

Fmaj9
3fr.
G
___ with you___ right___ now,___
the state that___ you're in.___

C
Dm7
I should be hold - ing you in - stead of los - ing my mind.
G
C/G
G7
Fmaj9
Just when you need me the most,
G
Am7
so does the coast. But I swear,
Dm7
Gsus4
G
C
To Coda
I'll make it up to you this time.

1.
Fmaj9
3fr.
G
C/G
G7
Am7add4
3fr.
B♭6/9
2.
C
D.S. al Coda
I should be
Coda
B♭6/9
Fsus2/A
G
C
rit.

from the
HEART

Alphabetical Listing

32 | Annie's Song

52 | Battle Hymn Of Love, The

56 | Calm At The Center Of My Storm, The

21 | Deeper Than The Holler

17 | Few Good Things Remain, A

94 | Forever And Ever, Amen

98 | Goin' Gone

102 | I Know Where Love Lives

114 | I Should Be With You

4 | I Swear

88 | I Won't Take Less Than Your Love

82 | I'll Leave This World Loving You

78 | Lady

72 | Like I Used To Do

69 | Lines Around Your Eyes

24 | Longer

12 | Love Can Build A Bridge

40 | Love Chooses You

36 | Love Is Strong

29 | Part Of Me

45 | She Is His Only Need

107 | This Shirt

60 | 'Til The Mountains Disappear

64 | Unanswered Prayers

8 | Where've You Been

Cherry Lane
Music
• Quality In Printed Music •